SAY HI TO EIFFEL!

Places To Go In France

Geography For Kids

Children's Explore The World Books

Speedy Publishing LLC

40 E. Main St. #1156

Newark, DE 19711

www.speedypublishing.com

Copyright 2017

All Rights reserved. No part of this book may be reproduced or used in any way or form or by any means whether electronic or mechanical, this means that you cannot record or photocopy any material ideas or tips that are provided in this book.

In this book, we're going to talk about places to visit in France. So, let's get right to it!

The country of France is one of the most beautiful in the world. There are so many amazing places to visit. There are castles that belong in fairy tales, towering cathedrals, and museums filled with art masterpieces. Let's start with the Eiffel Tower. It's an icon for France and especially the capital city of Paris, which is called "The City of Lights."

Eiffel Tower, Paris

Gustave Eiffel

THE EIFFEL TOWER

The majestic Eiffel Tower was created by Gustave Eiffel in 1889. It was only supposed to be a temporary structure for the world's fair, but became a symbol for the city of Paris. Originally many art and architecture critics didn't like it. It's an amazing feat of engineering with 8,000 parts made of metal.

The tower is 320 meters high and it's known as the "Iron Lady" because of its graceful, metallic curves. Visitors to the city are amazed by the tower's height and the incredible views of Paris that can be seen from three different levels. Looking out over the city on a clear day, you can see to a distance of 70 kilometers from the top level. The Eiffel Tower houses several restaurants with expensive, award-winning cuisine.

THE LOUVRE MUSEUM

The Louvre Museum is the largest and one of the most famous museums in the world. In fact, it's so large that you could be there for an entire week and not see everything! Its collection contains over 30,000 pieces of art, many of which are considered masterpieces.

Louvre at Paris

Entrance to Louvre Museum in Paris

It used to be a royal palace for the kings of France and they were the original collectors of many of the pieces. Some of the pieces were obtained because of France's treaties with the Republic of Venice as well as the Vatican. Many of the Egyptian pieces come from Napoleon's military campaigns.

The Louvre has a large, modern, transparent pyramid entrance that was added to the building in 1989. There are two smaller pyramids at the sides as well. The most famous painting housed in the Louvre is Leonardo Da Vinci's masterpiece the Mona Lisa painted between 1503 to 1506.

The Winged Victory of Samothrace

It's a small painting and many people are surprised by its size when they see it. The following is a list of a few of the museum's other famous works.

- The Nike of Samothrace, which is also called Winged Victory, was created around 190 BC. This beautiful Greek statue with its detailed wings and flowing garments would inspire anyone to win.

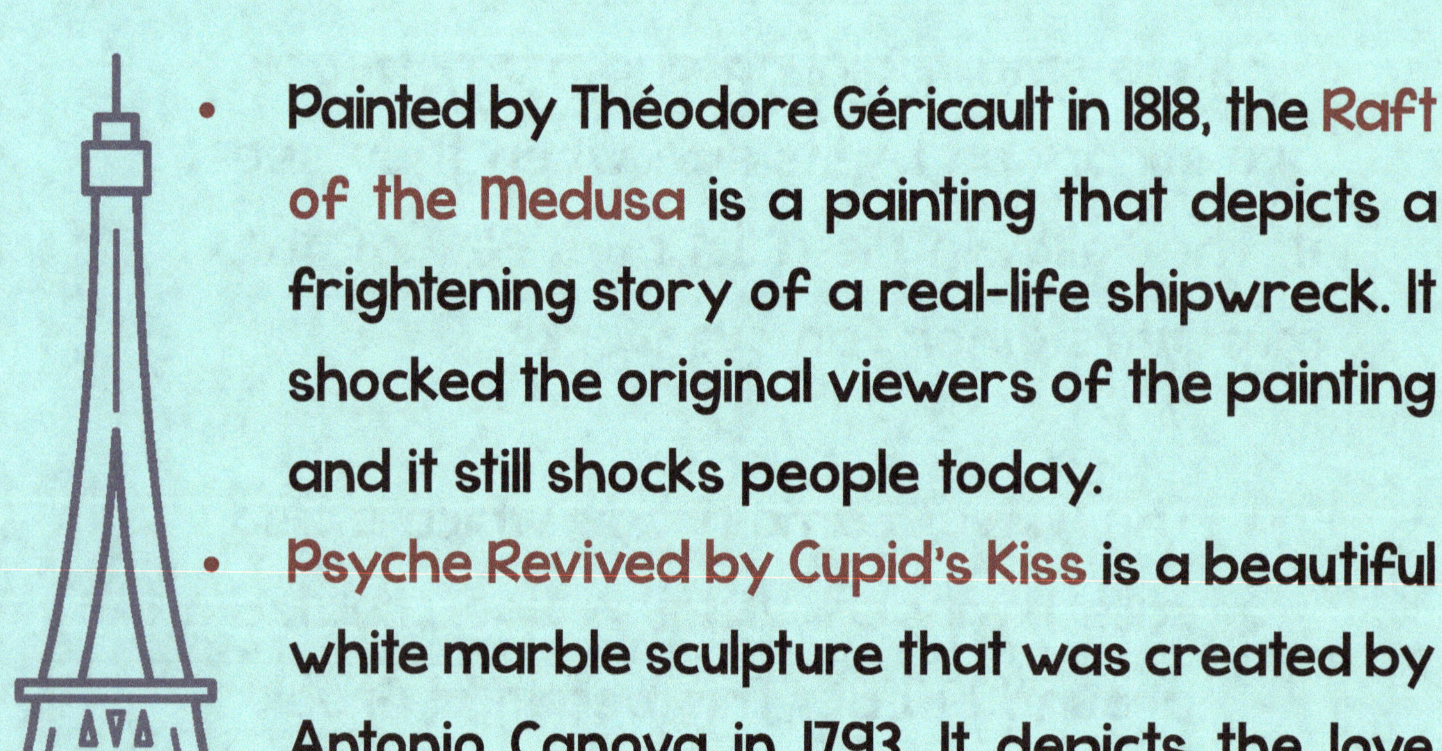

- Painted by Théodore Géricault in 1818, the Raft of the Medusa is a painting that depicts a frightening story of a real-life shipwreck. It shocked the original viewers of the painting and it still shocks people today.

- Psyche Revived by Cupid's Kiss is a beautiful white marble sculpture that was created by Antonio Canova in 1793. It depicts the love story of Cupid and Psyche.

Psyche Revived by Cupid's Kiss

Face of a Seated Scribe

- **The Seated Scribe** is a sculpture from the 4th dynasty in Egypt that was created around 2620 BC. It's considered to be one of the most important pieces in the Egyptian collection.

- The **Venus de Milo,** created around 130 BC, is a famous Greek sculpture depicting the goddess of love.

THE PALACE OF VERSAILLES

This royal palace was the home of King Louis XIV. He took his father's tiny hunting lodge and had it transformed into an amazing, elaborate palace. It had a façade as well as interior rooms designed using the Baroque style.

Versailles Palace facade and golden fence

Louis XIV

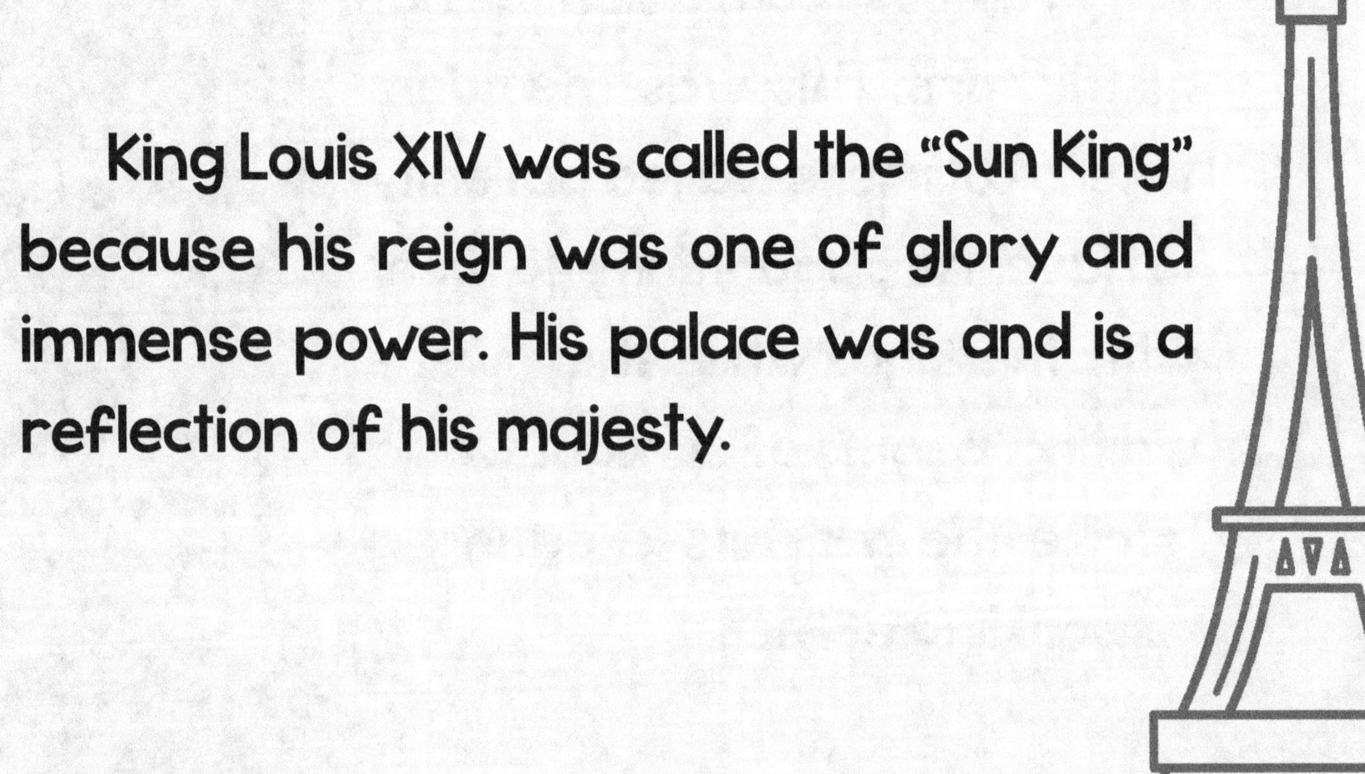

King Louis XIV was called the "Sun King" because his reign was one of glory and immense power. His palace was and is a reflection of his majesty.

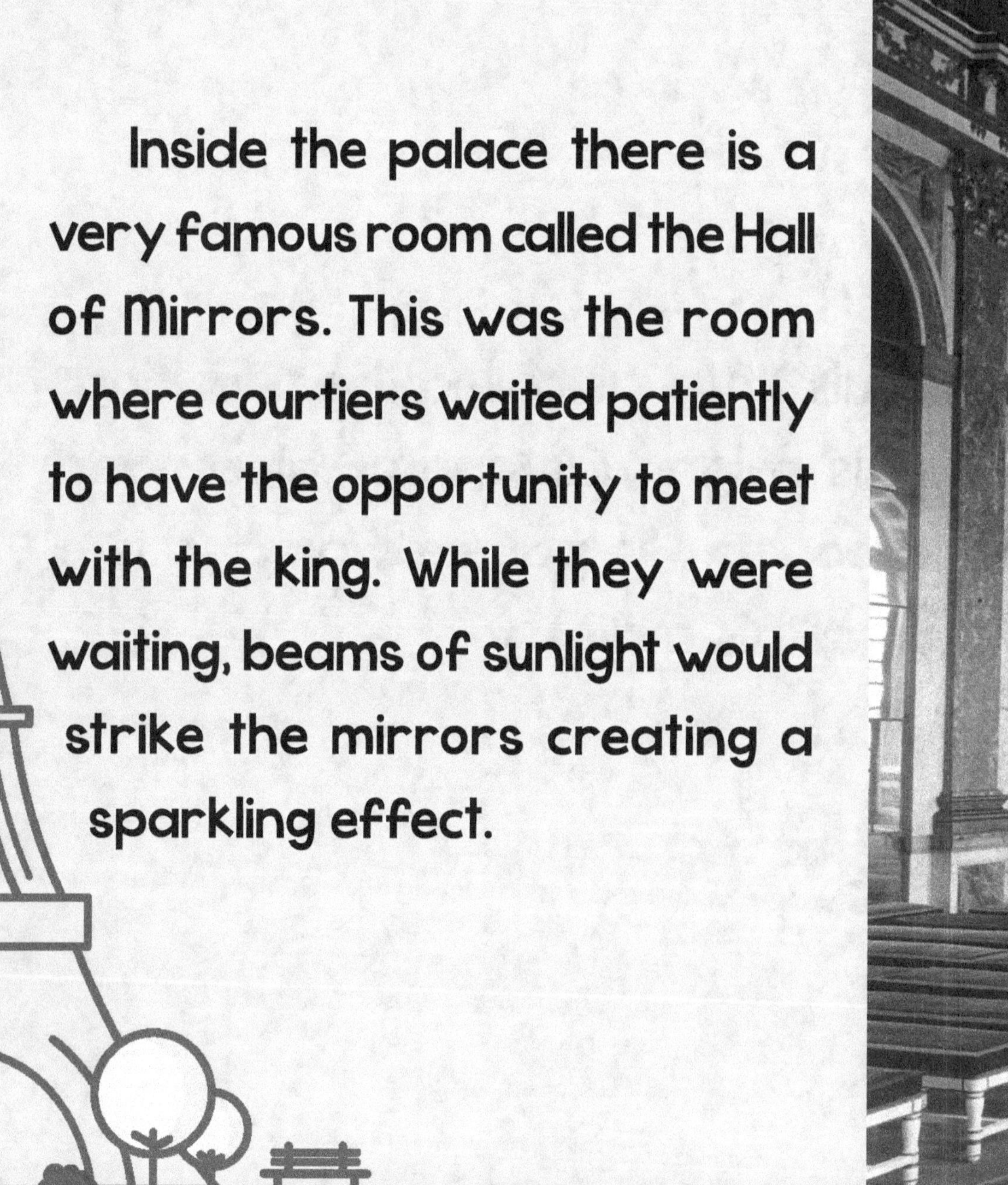

Inside the palace there is a very famous room called the Hall of Mirrors. This was the room where courtiers waited patiently to have the opportunity to meet with the king. While they were waiting, beams of sunlight would strike the mirrors creating a sparkling effect.

The palace is also known for its formal gardens with carefully placed pools surrounded by neatly trimmed shrubs. Nearby is a make-believe country village where Marie-Antoinette used to come and take long, relaxing walks to escape the tension of life at court.

THE CÔTE D'AZUR

The Côte d'Azur means the "blue coast" and is named after the Mediterranean Sea's deep blue color. This stretch of coast is also known as the French Riviera, which stretches from Saint-Tropez to the city of Menton, which is close to the Italian border.

Cote d'Azur France

The summertime brings throngs of visitors who want to bask on the beaches and "worship" the sun. Wealthy people vacation here in the huge villas and on their luxury yachts. Each city along the coast has something special to offer.

- Nice has amazing views of the sea and wonderful art museums.
- Cannes is known for its film festival when celebrities come to town and stay in the many luxurious hotels.

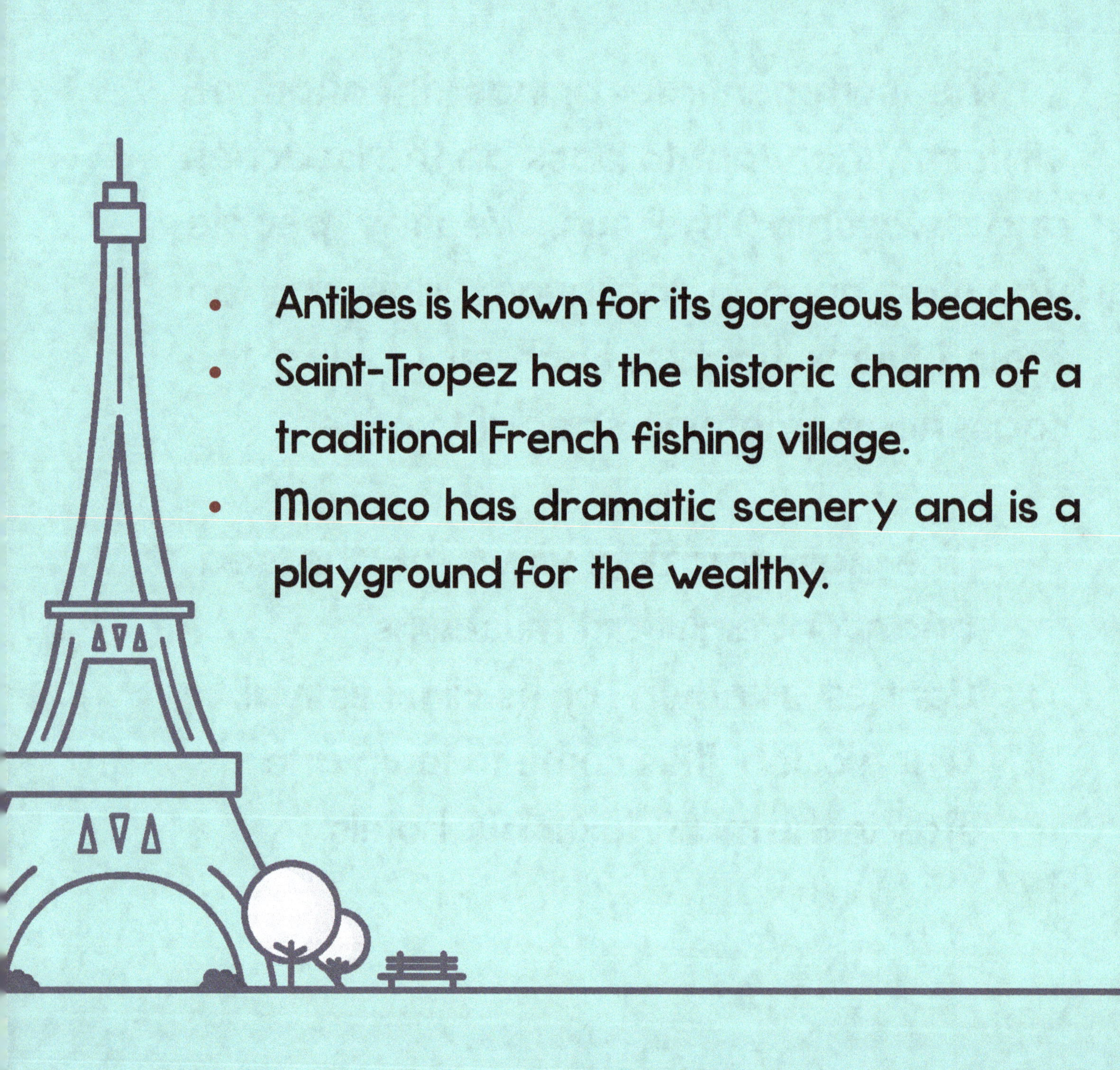

Antibes is known for its gorgeous beaches.

Saint-Tropez has the historic charm of a traditional French fishing village.

Monaco has dramatic scenery and is a playground for the wealthy.

Sailboats and yachts moored to the quay
port of Saint-Tropez, France

Mont St Michel

MONT SAINT-MICHEL

During high tide, Mont Saint-Michel rises out of the sea like a pyramid. The main attraction on the island is the Abbaye de Saint-Michel, which was built in 708 AD. The Archbishop Aubert of Avranches commissioned the structure, which stands at the peak of the island, after he had a vision of the Archangel Michael.

It's an amazing example of Gothic medieval architecture with spires that rise over 150 meters above the level of the sea. At low tide, visitors can walk across the sand to get to the island. Because the island is so serene and has a spiritual feeling it is often called "The Heavenly Jerusalem."

Loire Valley Châteaux

Visitors who travel in the Loire Valley feel as if they were traveling inside a fairy tale. The woodlands and valleys seem enchanted. The medieval castles have moats for protection and towers with turrets that look like tall, pointed hats.

Loire castle

Chambord castle

Named the "Garden of France," the Loire Valley has been designated as a UNESCO World Heritage Site. These beautiful castles were designed to help the king and his court relax and entertain outside of the city life in Paris. The most elaborate castle is the Château de Chambord, which was constructed for King Francis I. Two other famous castles are the Château de Chenoceau and the Cheverny.

CATHÉDRALE NOTRE-DAME DE CHARTRES

Although the Notre-Dame Cathedral in Paris is better known, many believe this cathedral in the city of Chartres is the best example of Gothic architecture in Europe. Built in the thirteenth century, this beautiful cathedral has been known to restore faith in those who doubted.

Notre Dame Cathedral

Rose window in Notre Dame Cathedral

The original stained glass windows are amazing feats of art and craftsmanship. The rose windows are especially breathtaking. From the month of April through the month of October, the city lights up the cathedral at night, which is a spectacular sight.

THE REGION OF PROVENCE

A region of southeastern France, Provence is a lovely landscape. There are groves of olives and rolling hills that bask in the sunlight. Small villages are tucked in the valleys and surrounded by fields of lavender.

Lavender field in the region of Provence

The Peppermint Bottle, by Paul Cezanne

It's no wonder that so many artists came to this naturally beautiful region to be inspired and create new types of innovative art. Some of the artists who worked in Provence and eventually became famous for their styles of art were:

- Cézanne, a great master of still life painting
- Matisse, master of a style of painting he created called Fauvism, which used vivid colors as well as flat spaces

- Chagall, who used bright colors as well as the techniques of Cubism and Fauvism
- Picasso, a pioneer of Cubism and one of the most famous artists of the 20th century

In Provence, visitors stroll leisurely along the streets of cobblestone. They're on their way to sit in the sun and enjoy cool drinks at the terraces of open-air cafés.

Courgettes
Extra
Nouvelles
du Chez Nous
1.50
France Nice
480
Poivrons

The food served there is a flavorful Mediterranean cuisine with garden-grown vegetables, pungent herbs, and olive oil. The town of Aix-en-Provence is known for its outdoor market. The town of Arles is popular for its ancient ruins as well as its fun festivals. Avignon is significant because of its medieval history. Even the smaller villages, such as Saint-Rémy, have wonderful museums, interesting historic sites to visit, and a quaint French country atmosphere.

MONT-BLANC

Mont Blanc is the tallest mountain peak on the European continent and is located on the border of France and Italy in the French Alps. At 4,810 meters tall, Mont Blanc, which translates to "White Mountain," is so tall that it always wears a blanket of snow. At its base is the lovely alpine village called Chamonix with its historic buildings, restaurant chalets, and quaint inns.

Mont Blanc mountain

SUMMARY

France is a beautiful, scenic country. From the awe-inspiring Gothic cathedrals to more modern marvels like the Eiffel Tower and the Louvre Pyramids, there are amazing feats of

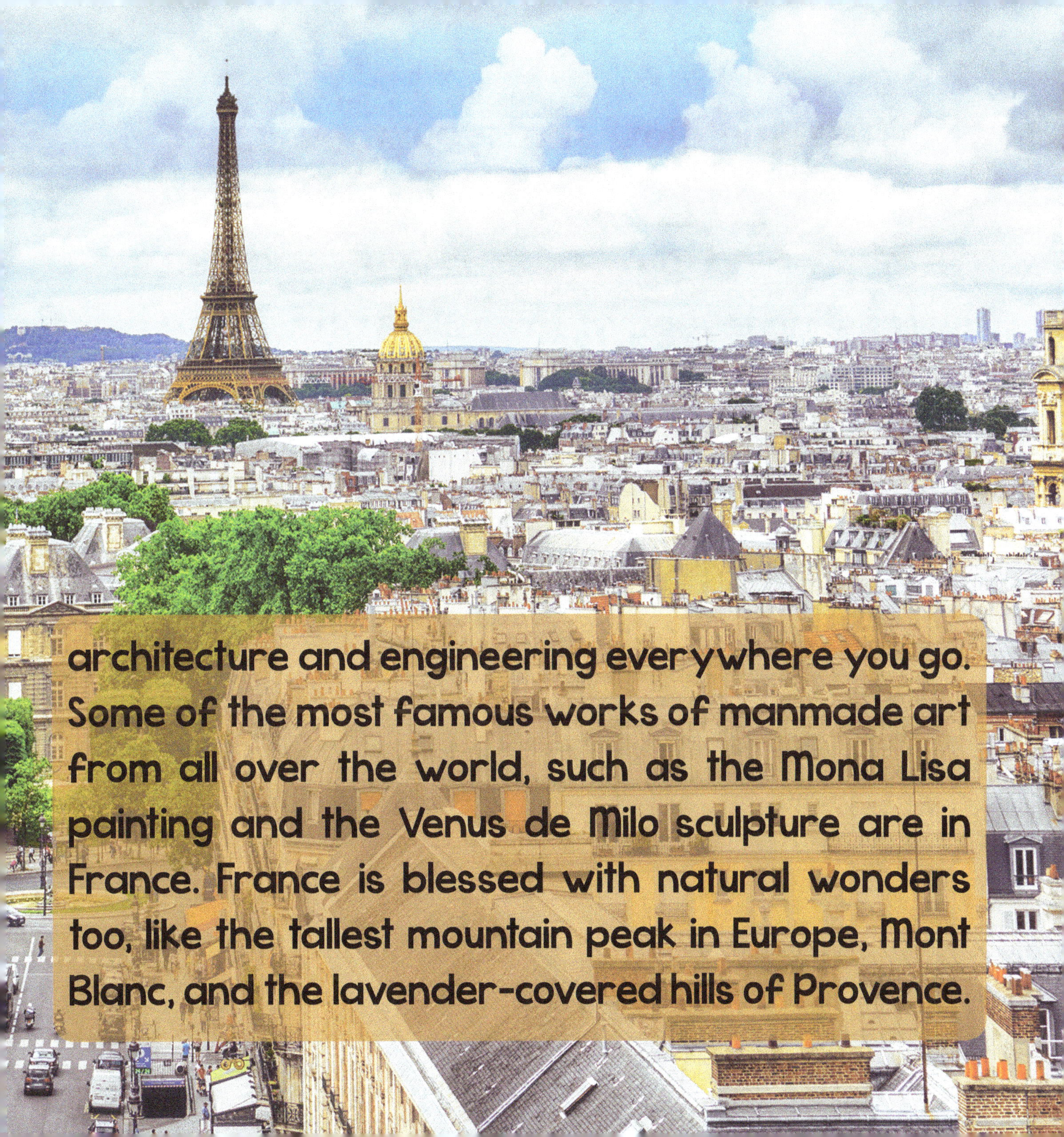

architecture and engineering everywhere you go. Some of the most famous works of manmade art from all over the world, such as the Mona Lisa painting and the Venus de Milo sculpture are in France. France is blessed with natural wonders too, like the tallest mountain peak in Europe, Mont Blanc, and the lavender-covered hills of Provence.

Awesome! Now that you know more about places to visit in France you may want to find out more about another interesting country to visit in the Baby Professor book **The Spices of Morocco: The Most Aromatic Country in Africa.**

Visit

BABY PROFESSOR
EDUCATION KIDS

www.BabyProfessorBooks.com

to download Free Baby Professor eBooks
and view our catalog of new and exciting
Children's Books

www.ingramcontent.com/pod-product-compliance
Lightning Source LLC
Chambersburg PA
CBHW081233130726

47997CB00009B/2864